CCSS **Genre** Fantasy

MW00364401

Essential Questi
What can stories t___ ___

Duck's Discovery

by May Kennedy
illustrated by Audrey Durney

Chapter 1
Curious Duck

Duck lived on a farm with Farmer Finn. The farm was in the middle of nowhere. It stretched for miles and miles.

Duck liked to know what was happening in the world.

She liked seeing new things.

She liked learning new things.

Duck liked to think she was curious.
After all, not many ducks wanted to know
why the sky was blue or why stars twinkled
at night.

She thought life was a journey of
discovery. Duck loved flying around and
looking at different people and places. Duck
felt that there were always new things to see
and learn.

Farmer Finn was nothing like Duck. He was not curious. He never wondered why the sky was blue or why stars twinkled at night.

But Farmer Finn was a kind person. He took great care of his animals. He talked to them. Sometimes he even sang to them.

All the farms in the area grew crops.

Farmer Finn put a lot of effort into growing good crops, but his plants usually drooped and died.

Last year, he grew rows and rows of lettuces, but they all went limp.

Chapter 2

Learning to Grow

One spring morning, Farmer Finn decided to concentrate on growing a new crop.

He opened his cookbook. Perhaps he would be inspired to grow something new.

"I love eating rice," said Farmer Finn to Duck. "I think I will grow rows and rows of rice."

Duck was worried.

She told Farmer Finn what she had seen on one of her journeys.

"Well," said Duck. "Last summer, I flew over Farmer Mac's farm. I saw him in the middle of one of his fields. He was scratching his head."

"What was wrong?" asked Farmer Finn.

"Farmer Mac had tried to grow rice," explained Duck. "But Farmer Mac was not educated about growing rice. He had to guess what to do."

Farmer Finn listened carefully.

"Did Farmer Mac make a good guess?" asked Farmer Finn.

"No, he didn't," replied Duck. "Our summers are hot and dry. I read in a book that rice likes warm and wet weather. Rice likes deep water in the fields. Farmer Mac's fields weren't wet. The plants dried up and died."

"Oh, dear," said Farmer Finn. "What did Farmer Mac do?"

"He sold his farm and moved to the city," explained Duck.

Now Farmer Finn was worried. He didn't want to move to the city. He liked being a farmer.

Luckily, Duck's story gave him an idea.

Chapter 3
A Journey of Discovery

Farmer Finn hoped that Duck would like his idea.

"How would you like to go on another journey?" he asked.

"That sounds wonderful," said Duck. "What do you want me to do?"

"I want you to fly over all the farms for miles around," explained Farmer Finn. "I want you to discover which crops grow well."

Duck liked the idea very much.

Later that morning, she set off. She flapped her wings and waved good-bye to Farmer Finn.

"Good luck, Duck!" he cried.

Duck flew low and slow. She quickly saw which crops grew well in those parts. For mile upon mile, field upon field, row upon row, all Duck could see were corn plants.

Then she saw a field of rice plants. The plants were all withered. They had dried out in the hot sun.

The farmer was staring at the dying plants.

Duck realized that the farmer hadn't learned from the mistakes of others.

"I can't wait to tell Farmer Finn what I have seen," said Duck. "What an amazing journey of discovery!"

Farmer Finn watched and waited for Duck to return. Before long, he heard a loud quack in the sky. Duck dived down to tell Farmer Finn what she had discovered.

"Well," said Farmer Finn eagerly, "which crops should we plant?"

"There is only one crop to grow," said Duck. "Corn is king in these parts."

Farmer Finn smiled. He just adored corn.

"Let's start planting then," he said.

So Farmer Finn dug row after row until his back ached, while Duck used her beak to plant the corn seeds.

Later, in the fall, the farm animals watched the first harvest. The corn was good and healthy, and Farmer Finn felt very satisfied. At last his farming skills had improved. He picked some golden corn and shared it with all the animals.

But Duck didn't fill up on corn. She was eager to go on another journey of discovery.

She wanted to know what to plant for winter!

Respond to Reading

Summarize

Use details from the text to summarize what you learned about what stories can teach you.

Character	
Wants or Needs	Feelings
Actions	Traits

Text Evidence

1. What kind of text is *Duck's Discovery*? How do you know? Genre

2. What words in the story describe Farmer Finn's character? Character

3. What words help you understand *withered* on page 12? Synonyms

4. Write what Duck's actions show about her character. Write About Reading

Compare Texts
Read a fable that tells us a story and
teaches us a lesson, too.

The Lion and the Fox

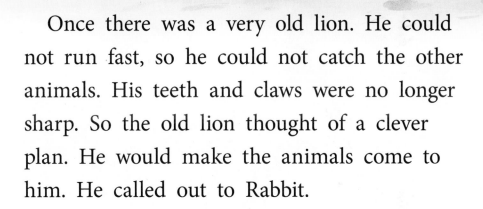

Once there was a very old lion. He could not run fast, so he could not catch the other animals. His teeth and claws were no longer sharp. So the old lion thought of a clever plan. He would make the animals come to him. He called out to Rabbit.

"Please help me, Rabbit. I am sick." When Rabbit came near his den, Lion gobbled him up.

Then he called out to Mouse and then Chicken. The foolish animals all fell for his plan. Lion gobbled them all up!

One day, a sly old fox stopped outside Lion's den.

"I hear that you are ill, Lion," said the fox. "What is wrong with you?"

"I can't hear you, Fox. You are too far away," said Lion. "Come closer."

But the fox was clever. He saw many animal footprints going into the den, but no prints came back out.

"Good try," said the fox. "But remember, foxes are tricksters, so I know a trick when I see one!"

The moral of the story is to learn from the mistakes of others.

Make Connections
What can we learn from stories?
Essential Question

Compare the ways that lessons are learned in each of these stories. Text To Text

Focus on
Genre

Fables Fables are written to teach us something important. They often have animals that can talk.

Read and Find In *The Lion and the Fox*, old Lion fools many animals. What is the lesson in this fable?

Your Turn

Plan a fable that uses a talking animal to teach a lesson. Make a story map to outline the characters, setting, and plot. Write a short description of each main character. Write some dialogue between the characters to show what is happening.

Character	Setting	Plot